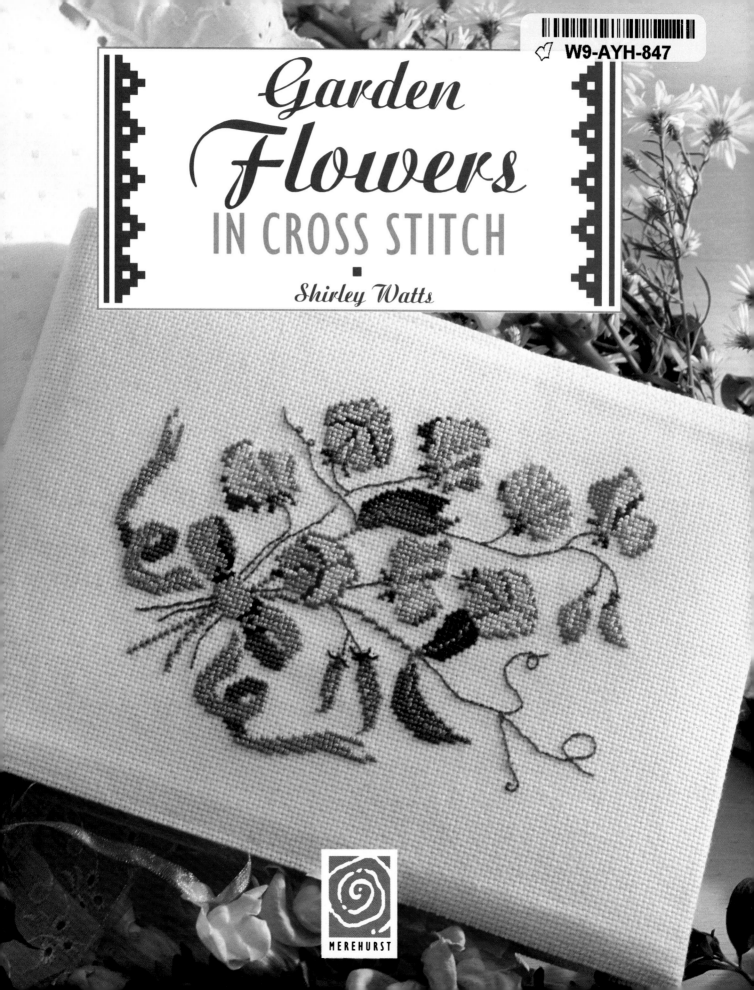

Garden Flowers
IN CROSS STITCH

Shirley Watts

MEREHURST

For Nancy, who loves her garden and all the flowers
that bloom so beautifully there.

THE CHARTS

Some of the designs in this book are very detailed and due to
inevitable space limitations, the charts may be shown on a
comparatively small scale; in such cases, readers may find it
helpful to have the particular chart with which they are
currently working enlarged.

THREADS

The projects in this book were all stitched with DMC stranded cotton
embroidery threads. The keys given with each chart also list thread
combinations for those who wish to use Anchor or Madeira threads.
It should be pointed out that the shades produced by different
companies vary slightly, and it is not always possible to find
identical colours in a different range.
Due to the difficulty of true photographic colour reproduction, the
threads recommended do not always match the photographs exactly.

Published in 1994 by Merehurst Limited
Ferry House, 51-57 Lacy Road, Putney, London SW15 1PR
Text © Copyright 1994 Shirley Watts
Photography and illustrations © Copyright 1994 Merehurst Limited
ISBN 1 85391 392 8

A catalogue record for this book is available from the British Library.

Managing Editor Heather Dewhurst
Edited by Diana Lodge
Designed by Maggie Aldred
Photography by Marie-Louise Avery
Illustrations by John Hutchinson
Typesetting by BMD Graphics, Hemel Hempstead
Colour separation by Fotographics Limited, UK – Hong Kong
Printed in Hong Kong by Wing King Tong

*Merehurst is the leading publisher of craft books and has an excellent range
of titles to suit all levels. Please send to the address above for our
free catalogue, stating the title of this book.*

CONTENTS

$\mathcal{I}$NTRODUCTION

'**G**od Almighty first planted a garden; and indeed it is the purest of human pleasures.' *Francis Bacon.*

A garden is a very special place. Whether it is neat and formal, a little untidy and on the wild side, or a pretty cottage garden, it invariably reflects the personality of the person who has created it. There can be few projects more rewarding then establishing a garden out of a chaotic, overgrown plot, and to see flowers blooming in a riot of colour. Whether we have a town patio, a bijou garden in the suburbs, or an estate in the country, we all have a favourite flower, and I hope that I have included some of your choices in this small collection.

I like to create my designs with live specimens in front of me, or failing that, from my own photographs. In this way, I try to capture the true spirit of the flower and make it as realistic as possible.

The projects vary in complexity: for those with little experience of cross stitch, there are floral cards and gift tags, and a number of smaller items to try, whilst for those looking for larger projects there is a cushion, a tea cosy and a selection of pictures.

The patterns have been worked on evenweave materials with between 22 and 14 threads or blocks per 2.5cm (1in). More experienced cross stitchers may like to work the designs on different counts from those suggested – to suit their eyesight – but in this case it is important to calculate the size of the completed design before beginning.

I hope that you enjoy stitching these designs, and that whatever time of year you do your stitching, they will bring some of the warmth and fragrance of summer into your home.

Happy stitching!

$\mathcal{B}$ASIC SKILLS

■

BEFORE YOU BEGIN

PREPARING THE FABRIC
Even with an average amount of handling, many evenweave fabrics tend to fray at the edges, so it is a good idea to overcast the raw edges, using ordinary sewing thread, before you begin.

THE INSTRUCTIONS
Each project begins with a full list of the materials that you will require; Aida, Tula, Lugana and Linda are all fabrics produced by Zweigart. Note that the measurements given for the embroidery fabric include a minimum of 3cm (1¼in) all around to allow for stretching it in a frame and preparing the edges to prevent them from fraying.

Colour keys for stranded embroidery cottons – DMC, Anchor or Madeira – are given with each chart. It is assumed that you will need to buy one skein of each colour mentioned, even though you may use less, but where two or more skeins are needed, this information is included in the main list of requirements.

To work from the charts, particularly those where several symbols are used in close proximity, some readers may find it helpful to have the chart enlarged so that the squares and symbols can be seen more easily. Many photocopying services will do this for a minimum charge.

Before you begin to embroider, always mark the centre of the design with two lines of basting stitches, one vertical and one horizontal, running from edge to edge of the fabric, as indicated by the arrows on the charts.

As you stitch, use the centre lines given on the chart and the basting threads on your fabric as reference points for counting the squares and threads to position your design accurately.

WORKING IN A HOOP
A hoop is the most popular frame for use with small areas of embroidery. It consists of two rings, one fitted inside the other; the outer ring usually has an adjustable screw attachment so that it can be tightened to hold the stretched fabric in place. Hoops are available in several sizes, ranging from

10cm (4in) in diameter to quilting hoops with a diameter of 38cm (15in). Hoops with table stands or floor stands attached are also available.

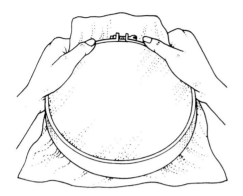

1 To stretch your fabric in a hoop, place the area to be embroidered over the inner ring and press the outer ring over it with the tension screw released. Tissue paper can be placed between the outer ring and the embroidery, so that the hoop does not mark the fabric. Lay the tissue paper over the fabric when you set it in the hoop, then tear away the central embroidery area.

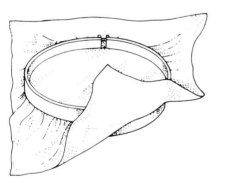

2 Smooth the fabric and, if needed, straighten the grain before tightening the screw. The fabric should be evenly stretched.

EXTENDING EMBROIDERY FABRIC
It is easy to extend a piece of embroidery fabric, such as a bookmark, to stretch it in a hoop.

● Fabric oddments of a similar weight can be used. Simply cut four pieces to size (in other words, to the measurement that will fit both the embroidery fabric and your hoop) and baste them to each side of the embroidery fabric before stretching it in the hoop in the usual way.

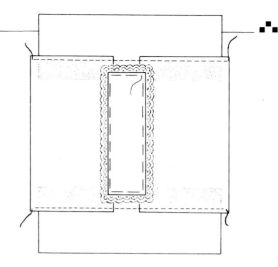

WORKING IN A RECTANGULAR FRAME
Rectangular frames are more suitable for larger pieces of embroidery. They consist of two rollers, with tapes attached, and two flat side pieces, which slot into the rollers and are held in place by pegs or screw attachments. Available in different sizes, either alone or with adjustable table or floor stands, frames are measured by the length of the roller tape, and range in size from 30cm (12in) to 68cm (27in).

As alternatives to a slate frame, canvas stretchers and the backs of old picture frames can be used. Provided there is sufficient extra fabric around the finished size of the embroidery, the edges can be turned under and simply attached with drawing pins (thumb tacks) or staples.

1 To stretch your fabric in a rectangular frame, cut out the fabric, allowing at least an extra 5cm (2in) all around the finished size of the embroidery. Baste a single 12mm (½in) turning on the top and bottom edges and oversew strong tape, 2.5cm (1in) wide, to the other two sides. Mark the centre line both ways with basting stitches. Working from the centre outwards and using strong thread, oversew the top and bottom edges to the roller tapes. Fit the side pieces into the slots, and roll any extra fabric on one roller until the fabric is taut.

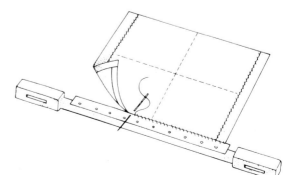

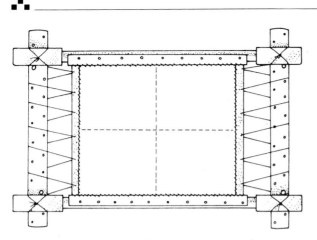

2 Insert the pegs or adjust the screw attachments to secure the frame. Thread a large-eyed needle (chenille needle) with strong thread or fine string and lace both edges, securing the ends around the intersections of the frame. Lace the webbing at 2.5cm (1in) intervals, stretching the fabric evenly.

ENLARGING A GRAPH PATTERN

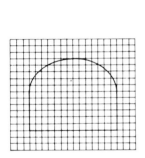
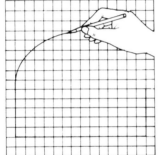

● To enlarge a graph pattern, you will need a sheet of graph paper ruled in 1cm (⅜in) squares, a ruler and pencil. If, for example, the scale is one square to 5cm (2in) you should first mark the appropriate lines to give a grid of the correct size. Copy the graph freehand from the small grid to the larger one, completing one square at a time. Use a ruler to draw the straight lines first, and then copy the freehand curves.

TO BIND AN EDGE

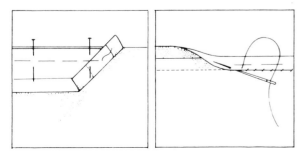

1 Open out the turning on one edge of the bias binding and pin in position on the right side of the fabric, matching the fold to the seamline. Fold over the cut end of the binding. Finish by overlapping the starting point by about 12mm (½in). Baste and machine stitch along the seamline.

2 Fold the binding over the raw edge to the wrong side, baste and, using matching sewing thread, neatly hem to finish.

PIPED SEAMS

Contrasting piping adds a special decorative finish to a seam and looks particularly attractive on items such as cushions and cosies.

You can cover piping cord with either bias-cut fabric of your choice or a bias binding; alternatively, ready-covered piping cord is available in several widths and many colours.

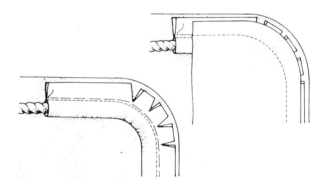

1 To apply piping, pin and baste it to the right side of the fabric, with seam lines matching. Clip into the seam allowance where necessary.

2 With right sides together, place the second piece of fabric on top, enclosing the piping. Baste and then either hand stitch in place or machine stitch, using a zipper foot. Stitch as close to the piping as possible, covering the first line of stitching.

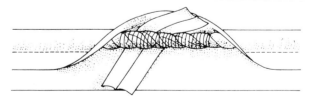

3 To join ends of piping cord together, first overlap the two ends by about 2.5cm (1in). Unpick the two cut ends of bias to reveal the cord. Join the bias strip as shown. Trim and press the seam open. Unravel and splice the two ends of the cord. Fold the bias strip over it, and finish basting around the edge.

MOUNTING EMBROIDERY

The cardboard should be cut to the size of the finished embroidery, with an extra 6mm (¼in) added all around to allow for the recess in the frame.

LIGHTWEIGHT FABRICS

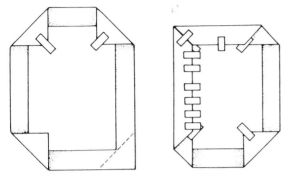

1 Place the emboidery face down, with the cardboard centred on top, and basting and pencil lines matching. Begin by folding over the fabric at each corner and securing it with masking tape.
2 Working first on one side and then the other, fold over the fabric on all sides and secure it firmly with pieces of masking tape, placed about 2.5cm (1in) apart. Also neaten the mitred corners with masking tape, pulling the fabric tightly to give a firm, smooth finish.

HEAVIER FABRICS

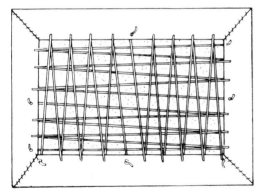

● Lay the embroidery face down, with the cardboard centred on top; fold over the edges of the fabric on opposite sides, making mitred folds at the corners, and lace across, using strong thread. Repeat on the other two sides. Finally, pull up the stitches fairly tightly to stretch the fabric firmly over the cardboard. Overstitch the mitred corners.

CROSS STITCH

For all cross stitch embroidery, the following two methods of working are used. In each case, neat rows of vertical stitches are produced on the back of the fabric.

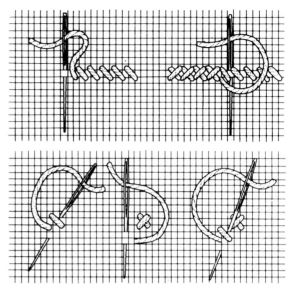

● When stitching large areas, work in horizontal rows. Working from right to left, complete the first row of evenly spaced diagonal stitches over the number of threads specified in the project instructions. Then, working from left to right, repeat the process. Continue in this way, making sure each stitch crosses in the same direction.
● When stitching diagonal lines, work downwards, completing each stitch before moving to the next.

BACKSTITCH

Backstitch is used in the projects to give emphasis to a particular foldline, an outline or a shadow. The stitches are worked over the same number of threads as the cross stitch, forming continuous straight or diagonal lines.

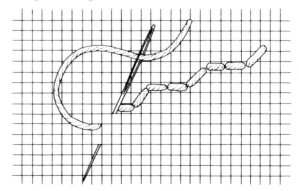

● Make the first stitch from left to right; pass the needle behind the fabric, and bring it out one stitch length ahead to the left. Repeat and continue in this way along the line.

Nasturtium Cushion

These brightly-coloured, climbing annuals bring the impression of sunshine into your garden, even on those dull days that can occur in summer. They are ideal for hanging baskets, patio containers and window boxes, for they are not only cheerful to look at, but are edible too.

NASTURTIUM CUSHION

YOU WILL NEED

For the Nasturtium Cushion Cover, measuring 41cm (16in) in diameter:

46cm (18in) square of cream, 14-count Aida fabric
46cm (18in) square of cream furnishing fabric, for the cushion back
Two 46cm (18in) squares of strong unbleached cotton fabric, for the inner cover
Stranded embroidery cotton in the colours given in the panel
No 24 tapestry needle
3.7m (4yds) of cream cushion cord, 6mm (¼in) in diameter
41cm (16in) cushion pad (or cushion filling, if preferred)

●

THE EMBROIDERY

Prepare the fabric by marking the centre lines with basting stitches. Start to embroider from the centre of the design. Use three strands of cotton in the needle for the cross stitch, and two strands for the backstitch. Steam press on the wrong side when complete.

MAKING UP THE COVER

After the embroidery is completed, use tailor's chalk to mark a 41cm (16in) circle on both pieces of cushion material – the Aida and the furnishing fabric. Pin them with right sides together, and machine around the edge, following the marked line and leaving a 25cm (10in) opening. Trim turnings to 12mm (½in), and turn right side out.

For the inner lining to contain the cushion pad or cushion filling, follow the same procedure.

Insert the pad or filling into the cushion lining, and stitch up the opening. Insert the covered pad into the embroidered cushion cover, and stitch up the opening.

Trim the edge of the cushion with the cord, making loops at intervals, as desired; slipstitch the cord in place.

NASTURTIUM ▶		DMC	ANCHOR	MADEIRA
⊥	Dark grey	844	401	1810
∷	Light grey	3022	8581	1903
•	Ecru	Ecru	926	Ecru
⊟	Light orange	741	304	0201
⊿	Deep yellow	972	298	0107
Z	Orange	971	316	0203
◣	Yellow	973	290	0105
‖	Bright yellow	307	289	0104
▼	Maroon	902	72	0601
∴	Red	349	46	0212
⊔	Light red	350	11	0213
⍁	Flame	608	330	0207
⊟	Peach	3340	328	0301
→	Dull red	347	13	0407
←	Dark orange	900	333	0208
H	Deep orange	946	332	0206
⊞	Bright orange	947	329	0205
✳	Dark green	935	862	1505
⎣	Green	580	267	1608
⎦	Yellowish green	581	266	1609
⊡	Bright green	907	255	1410
K	Light green	472	264	1414
⊞	Dull orange	721	324	0308
◠	Grey	646	273	1812
↑	Dark red	498	19	0511
⊟	Bright red	606	335	0209
	Black*	310	403	Black

Note: bks flower centres in black* (used for bks only), fringe on red flowers in dark red, fringe on yellow flowers in bright yellow, tendrils in either yellowish green or green (consult the photograph), basket in dark grey, fringe on orange flowers in dark orange, and fringe on salmon-coloured flowers in bright red.

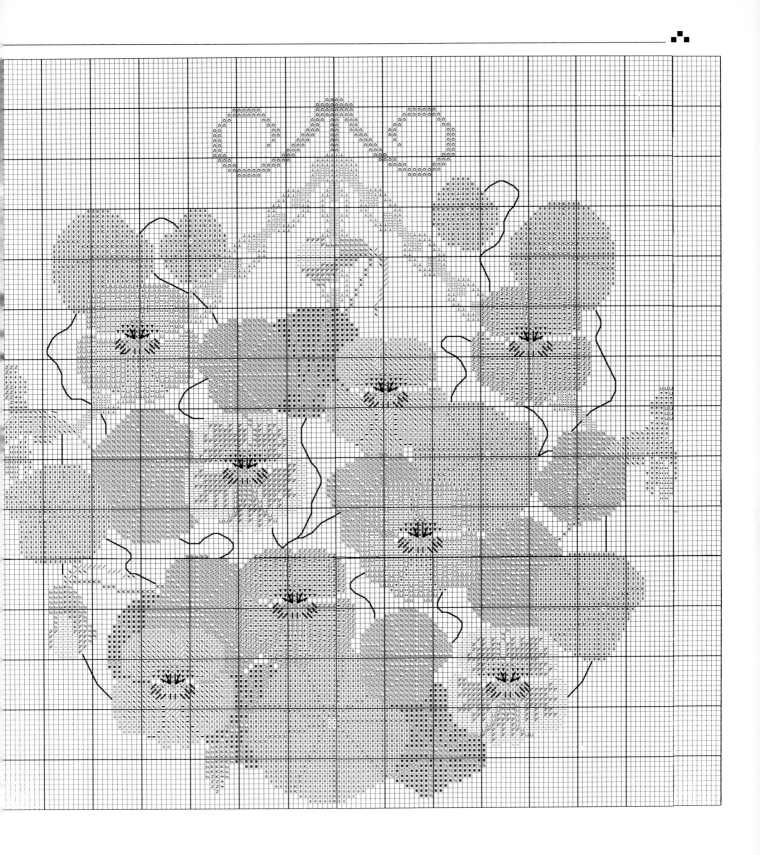

Tulip Picture

A favourite of Islamic artists and of
the Dutch masters, the tulip, which
originates from Asia Minor, is surely
one of the most elegant and varied
of cultivated flowers.
This pewter vase brim-full of striking
red and yellow tulips will bring a
breath of spring into your home.

TULIP PICTURE

YOU WILL NEED

For the Tulip Picture, mounted in a rectangular portrait frame, with an aperture measuring 25cm × 19.5cm (9¾in × 7¾in):

38cm × 33cm (15in × 13in) of cream, 18-count Aida fabric
Stranded embroidery cotton in the colours given in the panel
No 26 tapestry needle
Strong thread for lacing across the back when mounting
Stiff cardboard for mounting
Frame of your choice

•

THE EMBROIDERY

Prepare the fabric by marking the centre lines of the design with basting stitches. Start your embroidery from the centre of the design, completing the cross stitching first, and then the backstitching. Use two strands of thread for the cross stitch, and one strand for the backstitching.

Gently steam press the finished embroidery on the wrong side.

ASSEMBLING THE PICTURE

Trim the edges of the embroidery until it measures 34cm × 29cm (13½in × 11½in) and centre the picture over the cardboard mount.

Lace the embroidery over the mount, following the instructions on page 7, and complete the assembly of the frame according to the manufacturer's instructions.

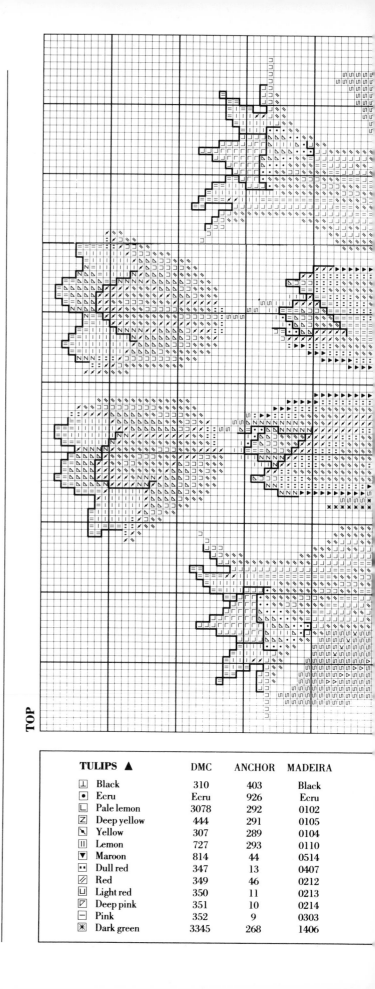

TOP

TULIPS ▲		DMC	ANCHOR	MADEIRA
⊥	Black	310	403	Black
•	Ecru	Ecru	926	Ecru
∟	Pale lemon	3078	292	0102
☑	Deep yellow	444	291	0105
◣	Yellow	307	289	0104
‖	Lemon	727	293	0110
▼	Maroon	814	44	0514
••	Dull red	347	13	0407
⊿	Red	349	46	0212
⊔	Light red	350	11	0213
▽	Deep pink	351	10	0214
⊟	Pink	352	9	0303
✳	Dark green	3345	268	1406

BOTTOM

		DMC	ANCHOR	MADEIRA
⑤	Bright green	987	244	1403
▽	Green	989	242	1401
⨮	Light green	3364	260	1603
◉	Dull green	3363	262	1602
÷	Mid green	3347	266	1408
ⓚ	Pale green	3348	265	1409
⊟	Dark grey	645	815	1811
◩	Medium grey	647	8581	1813
▽	Light grey	648	900	1814
⊠	Pale grey	762	234	1804
⊐	Light maroon	815	43	0513
⊓	Pale pink	353	8	0304
	Gold*	742	303	0107

Note: bks outline the two outer petals of the two central tulips in light maroon; the inner petals of the two central tulips, the bent-down petals of the two outer tulips and the front petals of the two upper tulips in dull red; around the tops of the petals of the two upper and the two outside tulips in gold* (used for bks only), and the shading under the vase in dull green.

15

Garden Border Picture

What could be lovelier than a bed of deep-scented hyacinths set against a terrace wall, spilling over with delicate pink and mauve aubrieta? Add a background of golden yellow forsythia and rose-coloured flowering currant, and winter is soon forgotten.

GARDEN BORDER PICTURE

YOU WILL NEED

For the Garden Border picture, mounted in a rectangular portrait frame, with an aperture measuring 22cm × 17cm (8¾in × 6¾in):

34cm × 30.5cm (13½in × 12in) of cream, 18-count Aida fabric
Stranded embroidery cotton in the colours given in the panel
No26 tapestry needle
Strong thread for lacing across the back when mounting
Stiff cardboard for mounting
Frame of your choice

•

THE EMBROIDERY

Prepare the fabric, marking the centre lines of the design with basting stitches. Start your embroidery from the centre of the design, completing the cross stitching first, and then the backstitching. Use two strands of thread for both the cross stitch and the backstitch.

Gently steam press the finished embroidery on the wrong side.

ASSEMBLING THE PICTURE

Trim the edges of the embroidery until it measures 31cm × 26cm (12¼in × 10¼in) and centre the picture over the cardboard mount.

Lace the embroidery over the mount, following the instructions on page 7, and complete the assembly according to the manufacturer's instructions.

TOP

BORDER ▲		DMC	ANCHOR	MADEIRA			DMC	ANCHOR	MADEIRA
⊥	Dark grey	413	401	1713	▲	Dark blue	792	940	0905
∷	Grey	647	8581	1813	△	Blue	793	121	0906
•	Pale grey	648	900	1814	◺	Pale blue	794	175	0907
⊞	Brown	610	889	2106	⊞	Light reddish brown	356	5975	0402
▬	Reddish brown	355	341	0401	⊞	Pinkish brown	758	868	0403
∕	Pale lemon	746	275	0101	■	Dark green	3363	262	1602
Z	Yellowish brown	676	891	2208	▣	Green	3364	260	1603
◤	Lemon	744	301	0112	÷	Lime green	472	264	1414
T	Dark mauve	552	101	0713	◆	Golden brown	435	365	2010
▫	Mauve	554	96	0711	⊟	Fawn	422	372	2102
◣	Pale mauve	211	342	0801	◹	Light golden brown	436	363	2011

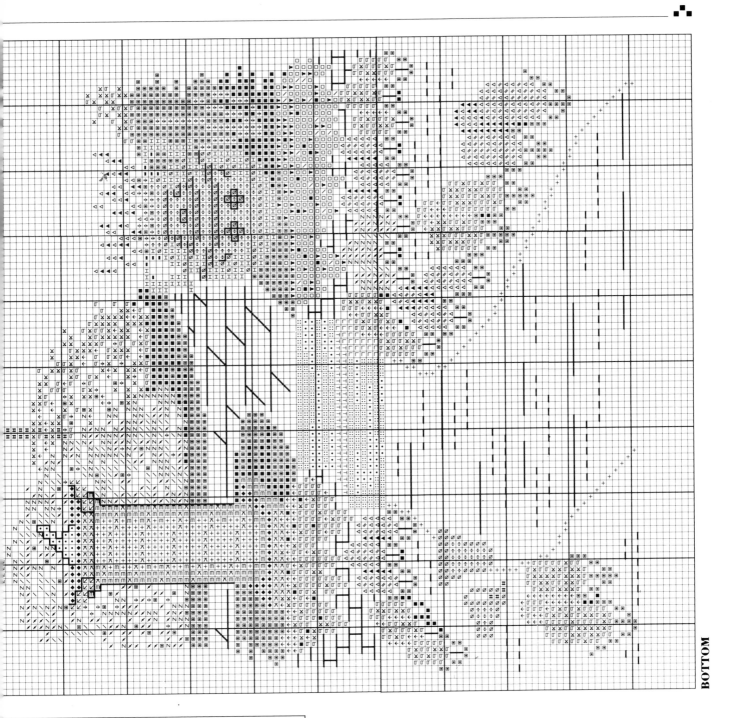

BOTTOM

		DMC	ANCHOR	MADEIRA
◨	Brownish pink	3064	914	2312
+	Light fawn	738	942	2013
⋈	Creamy fawn	739	885	2014
⊓	Silver grey	762	234	1804
↑	Deep pink	3607	87	0708
⊟	Pink	3608	86	0709
⊠	Pale pink	3609	85	0710

Note: bks soil and tree twigs in brown, all paving slabs (front and back paths) in light fawn, sundial and wall in grey, and terracotta pot in reddish brown; the hyacinth stems are stitched in green and dark green – green for the stems in the foreground, and dark green for the background stems, as seen in the photograph.

Flowers in Oval Frames

The pendulous golden blooms of laburnum and the delicate pale mauve of wistaria, which can make such a stunning combination growing against a wall, here complement each other in this pair of oval walnut frames.

FLOWERS IN OVAL FRAMES

YOU WILL NEED

For each Flower Picture, mounted in an
oval portrait frame, with an aperture
measuring 14cm × 9.5cm (5½in × 3¾in):

*20cm × 15cm (8in × 6in) of cream,
18-count Aida fabric
Stranded embroidery cotton in the colours given in
the panel
No 26 tapestry needle
Strong thread for lacing across the back when
mounting
Stiff cardboard for mounting
Frame of your choice*

•

THE EMBROIDERY

For each picture, prepare the fabric, marking the
centre lines of the design with basting stitches.
Start your embroidery from the centre of the design,
completing the cross stitching first, and then the
backstitching. Use two strands of thread for both
the cross stitch and the backstitching, except when
outlining the laburnum flowers, for which one
strand is used. Gently steam press the finished
embroidery on the wrong side.

ASSEMBLING THE PICTURE

Each picture is assembled in the same way. Trim
the edges of the embroidery until it measures
19cm × 14cm (7½in × 5½in) and centre the
picture over the cardboard mounting.

Lace the embroidery over the mount, following the
instructions on page 7, and complete the assembly
according to the manufacturer's instructions.

LABURNUM ▼		DMC	ANCHOR	MADEIRA
⊟	Brown	610	889	2106
Z	Deep yellow	444	291	0105
◣	Yellow	307	289	0104
⊏	Dark green	3362	862	1601
⊔	Pale green	472	264	1414
⊡	Green	3347	266	1408
K	Light green	3348	265	1409
+	Yellow green	734	279	1610
⊠	Lemon	445	288	0103

*Note: bks twig in brown, the stems of the two dark leaves and the
vein of the leaf worked in green in dark green, and all other stems
and leaves in green.*

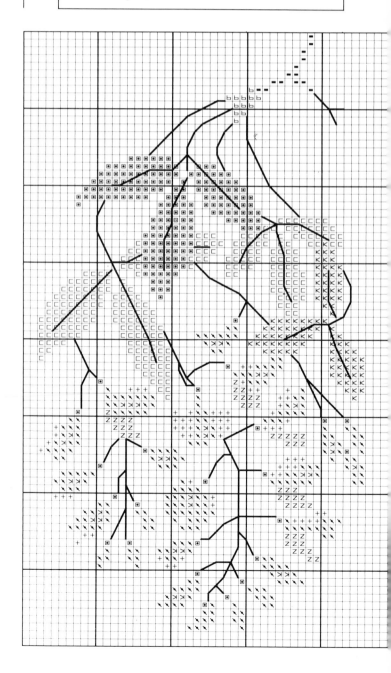

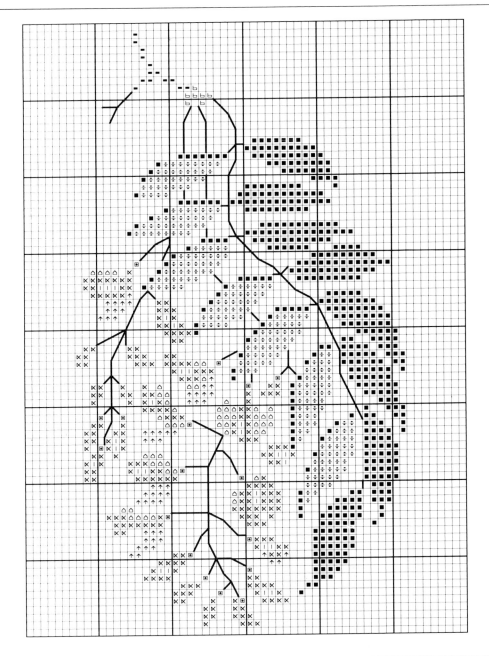

WISTARIA ▲		DMC	ANCHOR	MADEIRA
⊟	Brown	610	889	2106
⊔	Pale green	472	264	1414
■	Dark green	3346	817	1407
⊡	Green	3347	266	1408
÷	Yellowy green	470	267	1502
△	Dull mauve	3041	871	0806
↑	Deep mauve	208	110	0804
⊠	Mauve	210	108	0802
Ɩ	Pale mauve	211	342	0801

Note: bks the twig in brown and all other stalks in green.

Nightdress Case

Sleep-inducing poppies have been chosen to decorate this pretty nightdress case – not the usual red ones, but the soft and delicate blues of the Himalayan poppy, *Meconopsis grandis*.

NIGHTDRESS CASE

YOU WILL NEED

For the Nightdress Case, measuring 35cm (13¾in) square (exclusive of broderie anglaise), with an inset for embroidery of cream, 18-count Aida fabric, measuring 18cm (7in) square:

Stranded embroidery cotton in the colours given in the panel
No26 tapestry needle
Nightdress or cushion case, available from needlework shops

•

THE EMBROIDERY

Find the centre point on your square of Aida and, beginning at the centre of the pattern, embroider the blue poppy motif, using two strands of cotton in the needle for the cross stitch and one strand of cotton for the backstitch. Steam press on the wrong side.

TO COMPLETE THE CASE

Handstitch the remaining three sides of the inset embroidered panel into place.

MECONOPSIS ▶		DMC	ANCHOR	MADEIRA
⊡	Cream	746	275	0101
☐	Grey blue	931	921	1711
△	Deep turquoise	518	168	1106
○	Turquoise	519	167	1105
✕	Pale blue	775	128	1001
∧	Blue	334	145	1003
−	Pink	3689	49	0607
⊞	Orange	721	324	0308
⊹	Light orange	722	323	0307
⊔	Green	3053	859	1510
■	Dark green	3051	861	1508
⊡	Mid green	3052	860	1509
÷	Pale green	3348	265	1409
⊠	Yellowish green	472	264	1414
+	Yellowish brown	676	891	2208
⊠	Pale yellow	745	300	0111
	Black*	310	403	Black

Note: bks the centre and back of the flowers in black* (used for bks only).

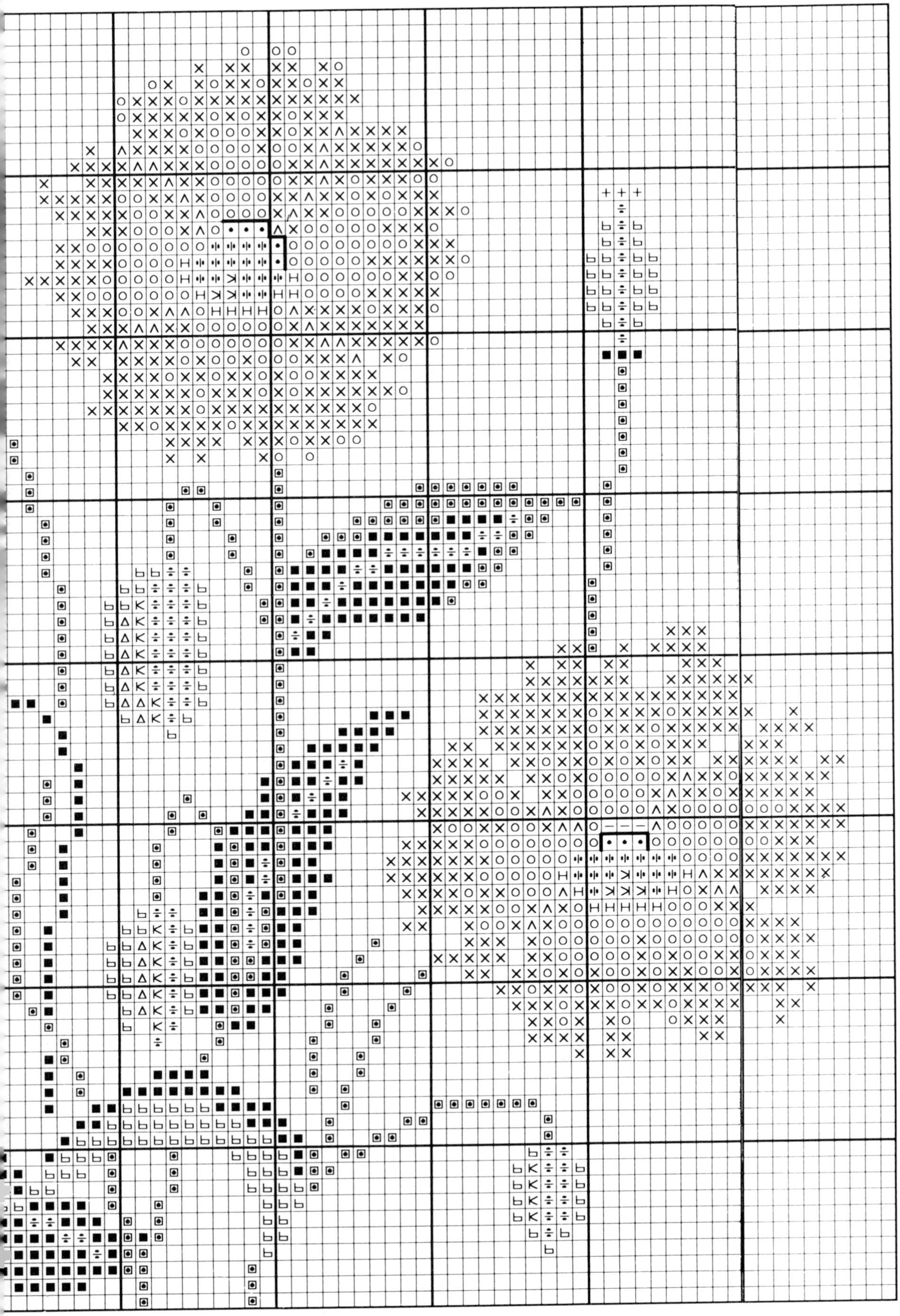

Periwinkle Table Set

This place setting and matching napkin are decorated with an attractive periwinkle design and will enhance any dining table.

PERIWINKLE TABLE SET

YOU WILL NEED

For one Placemat, measuring 46cm × 34cm
(18½in × 13½in):

*50cm × 39cm (20in × 15½in) of cream, 28-count
evenweave fabric
Stranded embroidery cotton in the colours given
in the panel
No 26 tapestry needle*

For one Napkin, measuring 37cm (14½in)
square:

*42cm (16½in) square of cream, 28-count
evenweave fabric
Stranded embroidery cotton in the colours given
in the panel
No 26 tapestry needle*

*NOTE: alternatively, ready-made placemats and
napkins can be obtained from specialist suppliers
(see page 48)*

For the Place Setting Card, measuring
9cm × 4cm (3½in × 1½in):

*5cm (2in) square of 22-count Hardanger fabric
Stranded embroidery cotton in the colours given
in the panel
No 26 tapestry needle
Card, obtainable from specialist suppliers (see
page 48)*

•

PLACEMAT AND NAPKIN

For the placemat, mark the central horizontal line
across the fabric with a line of basting stitches.
From the left-hand side of the fabric, measure in
along this line for 10cm (4in). A vertical line at this
point marks the centre, from which you should start
your embroidered panel, which is made up of two
complete motifs, one on each side of the horizontal
line.

For the napkin, which features only one motif,
baste a vertical line 10cm (4in) in from the left-
hand side and a horizontal one 13.5cm (5¼in) up
from the lower edge. The centre of the motif is the
point where these two lines intersect.

For both the placemat and the napkin, use three
strands of embroidery cotton in the needle for the

cross stitch and the backstitching of the stems. Use
only two threads in the needle for backstitching the
fine detail on the flower centre and petals. Work
over two fabric threads.

Gently steam press the finished embroideries on
the wrong side.

FRINGING

Trim 2.5cm (1in) all around the finished embroideries, so that the placemat measures 46cm × 34cm
(18½in × 13½in) and the napkin measures 37cm
(14½in) square.

On all four sides of each, withdraw a single
fabric thread 12mm (½in) in from the outer edge.

The fringing can be secured in one of several
ways; by machining around the rectangle (placemat) or square (napkin) left by the withdrawn
threads, using either straight stitch or narrow zigzag
stitch, or by overcasting every alternate thread
by hand.

When you have secured the line by your chosen
method, remove all cross threads below the stitched
line to complete the fringe. Alternatively, if a more
hard-wearing edge is preferred, a hemstitched hem
can be used instead of fringing.

PLACE SETTING CARD

Find the centre of the small square of Hardanger,
and using only one strand of embroidery cotton,
work a single periwinkle flower. Steam press on the
wrong side.

Mount the embroidery in the card, following the
manufacturer's instructions.

PERIWINKLE ▶		DMC	ANCHOR	MADEIRA
⊡	Pale mauve	211	342	0801
◩	Yellow	726	295	0109
⊏	Dark green	3363	262	1602
⊠	Green	3347	266	1408
⊟	Bright green	989	242	1401
÷	Pale green	3364	260	1603
⊐	Dark purple	550	102	0714
⊥	Purple	208	110	0804
△	Dark mauve	209	109	0803
⊓	Mauve	210	108	0802
	White*	Blanc	White	White

*Note: bks stems in pale green, flower centres in dark green, and
flower petals in white* (used for bks only).*

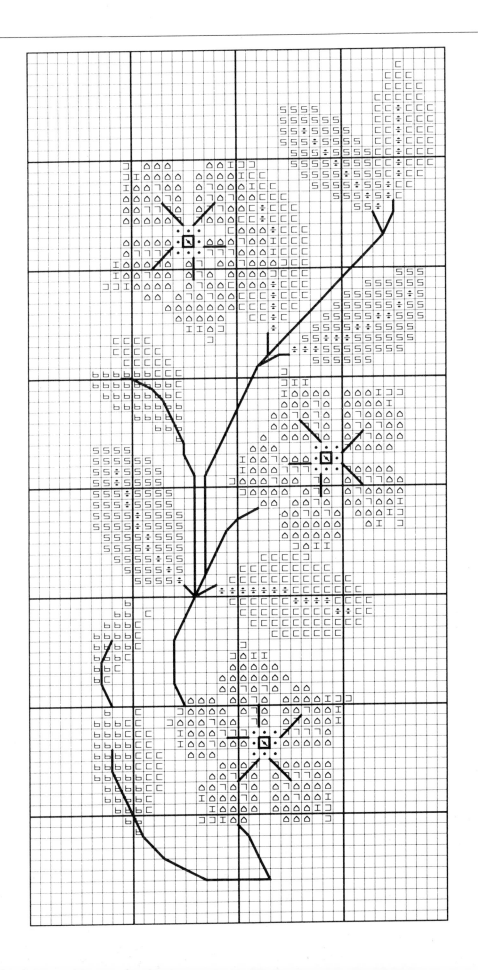

Photograph Album and Pillow

For that christening present with a difference, here is an easy-to-make cover for an album of treasured photographs. The cover is decorated with delicate, pastel-shaded sweet peas. To complement this, why not embroider a baby's pillow with matching flowers?

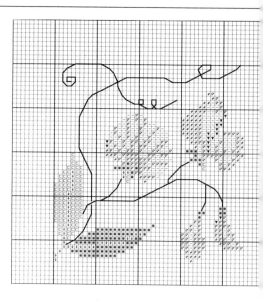

PHOTOGRAPH ALBUM AND PILLOW

YOU WILL NEED

For the cover to fit a baby's Photograph Album, measuring 21.5cm × 16cm (8½in × 6¼in):

68cm × 19cm (27in × 7½in) of cream, 18-count Aida fabric
47cm × 16.5cm (18½in × 6½in) of white interfacing
Stranded embroidery cotton in the colours given in the panel
No 26 tapestry needle

For the baby's Pillow Cover, measuring 33cm (13in) square, including the broderie anglaise edging:

12.5cm (5in) square of white, 18-count Aida fabric, for the embroidered motif
32cm (12½in) square of white damask, for the front of the pillow
28cm × 32cm (11in × 12½in) and another strip 10cm × 32cm (4in × 12½in), both of white damask, for the back of the pillow
1.8m (1¾yds) of frilled insertion broderie anglaise, 5cm (2in) wide
1.8m (1¾yds) of pink or blue ribbon, of an appropriate width to slot through your broderie anglaise
Stranded embroidery cotton in the colours given in the panel
No 26 tapestry needle

●

THE ALBUM COVER

Fold the Aida in half, giving you a working area 34cm × 19cm (13½in × 7½in). With the fold on the left, measure in 19mm (¾in) from the fold and baste from top to bottom. From this line, measure a further 21.5cm (8½in) across and baste another line from top to bottom. From the top edge, measure down 15mm (⅔in) and from the bottom edge measure up 15mm (⅔in). Baste along these two lines. This will leave you with a rectangular area 21.5cm × 16cm (8½in × 6¼in) for the front cover of your album.

Position your embroidery either centrally within this area or slightly towards the bottom left-hand corner, whichever you prefer. Use two strands of cotton for the cross stitch, two strands for back-

stitching the stalks and tendrils, and one strand for backstitching the fine detail on the seed pods.

Gently steam press on the wrong side when complete.

MAKING UP THE COVER

Centre the interfacing lengthwise on the Aida fabric. Fold the Aida to form a narrow hem along all the edges, enclosing the interfacing, and machine stitch in position. Centre the album on the wrong side of the fabric and fold the extra width over the front and over the back cover. Seam along the edges at the top and bottom to form a pocket at the front and back.

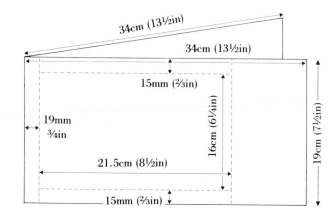

BABY'S PILLOW COVER

Find the centre point of your square of Aida and, beginning from the centre of the pattern, embroider the sweet pea motif, using two strands of cotton in the needle, both for the cross stitch and for the backstitch. The sample has been worked in pink, but alternative shades of blue are given in the key to the motif design. Gently steam press on the wrong side when complete.

SWEET PEA PILLOW ◄	DMC	ANCHOR	MADEIRA
▼ Maroon	902	72	0601
▨ Deep pink	602	63	0702
▷ Pink	603	62	0701
⊟ Pale pink	605	60	0613
⊏ Dark green	3345	268	1406
▣ Green	3346	817	1407
⊹ Light green	3347	266	1408
Alternative blue shaded for boy			
▼ Dark blue	333	119	0903
▨ Blue	340	118	0902
▷ Light mauve	210	108	0802
⊟ Pale mauve	211	342	0801
⊏ Dark green	3345	268	1406
▣ Green	3346	817	1407
⊹ Light green	3347	266	1408

Note: whether the pillow is for a boy or girl, bks flower stalk in green and tendrils in dark green.

SWEET PEA ALBUM COVER ▼	DMC	ANCHOR	MADEIRA
⊤ Black	310	403	Black
▼ Dark blue	333	119	0903
▢ Navy	939	127	1009
◇ Blue	340	118	0902
◳ Pale blue	341	117	0901
▼ Maroon	902	72	0601
▨ Deep pink	602	63	0702
▷ Pink	603	62	0701
⊟ Pale pink	605	60	0613
✳ Dark green	3345	268	1406
⑤ Medium green	3346	817	1407
⊡ Green	3347	266	1408
⊠ Yellowish green	472	264	1414
⊐ Purple	208	110	0804
⊥ Mauve	209	109	0803
⌂ Light mauve	210	108	0802
⊓ Pale mauve	211	342	0801
↑ Reddish purple	550	102	0714

Note: bks all branches and tendrils in medium green, and the calyx of the pea pods in dark green.

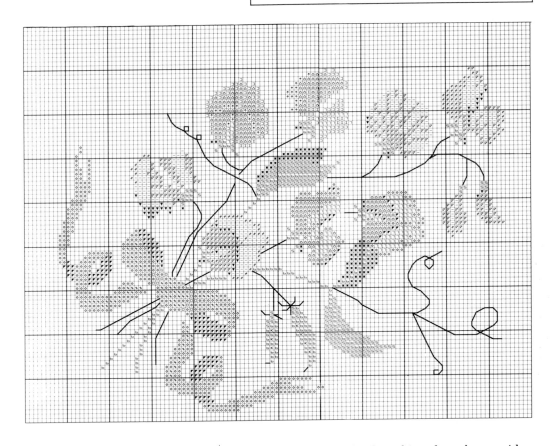

MAKING UP THE PILLOW

Make a narrow hem on one of the 32cm (12½in) sides of the larger back piece of the damask, and repeat on one of the 32cm (12½in) sides of the narrow strip.

Cut a 9cm (3½in) square from the top left corner of the front piece of damask, and snip the inner corner of the cut area to facilitate the turning of a 6mm (¼in) hem along the two cut sides. Insert the embroidered motif and machine along the two sides.

With all right sides together, place the back piece of damask on the larger front piece and then the narrower strip, overlapping the two. Machine around all four sides. Turn right side out and press.

Machine the broderie anglaise into place all around the pillow on the extreme edge, mitring the corners. Slip a ready-made cot or pram pillow into the finished cover.

Floral Correspondence

Any keen gardener or flower-arranger would be happy to receive one of these cross-stitched greetings cards or a gift with a hand-embroidered tag, depicting a vibrant orange lily, or the more exotic passion flower.

FLORAL CORRESPONDENCE

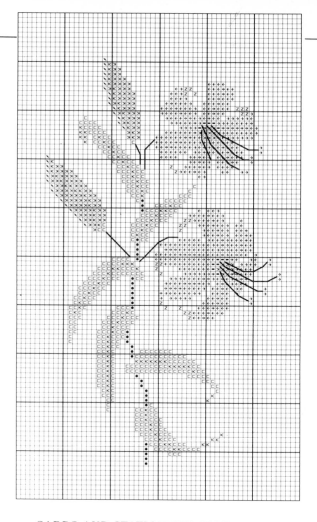

YOU WILL NEED

For the Lily Card, measuring 20.5cm × 15cm (8in × 6in), with an oval portrait cut-out measuring 14cm × 9cm (5½in × 3½in):

19cm × 14cm (7½in × 5½in) of cream, 18-count Aida fabric
19cm × 14cm (7½in × 5½in) of iron-on interfacing
Stranded embroidery cotton in the colours given in the panel
No 26 tapestry needle
Greetings card, for suppliers see page 48

For the Passion Flower Card, measuring 20.5cm × 15cm (8in × 6in), with an oval portrait cut-out, measuring 14cm × 9cm (5½in × 3½in):

19cm × 14cm (7½in × 5½in) of eau-de-Nil, 18-count Aida fabric
19cm × 14cm (7½in × 5½in) of iron-on interfacing
Stranded embroidery cotton in the colours given in the panel
No 26 tapestry needle
Greetings card, for suppliers see page 48

For the *Lavatera* Stationery Compendium, measuring 21.5cm × 15cm (8½ × 6in), with an oval portrait cut-out measuring 16cm × 10cm (6½in × 4in):

20cm × 14cm (8in × 5½in) of cream, 18-count Aida fabric
20cm × 14cm (8in × 5½in) of iron-on interfacing
Stranded embroidery cotton in the colours given in the panel
No 26 tapestry needle
Stationery set, from good needlework shops

For each Gift Tag, with an overall measurement of 12cm × 5cm (5in × 2in), folded to give a front panel 5cm (2in) square, with a cut-out 4cm (1½in) in diameter:

6.5cm (2½in) square of cream, 22-count Hardanger
6.5cm (2½in) square of iron-on interfacing
Stranded embroidery cotton in the colours given in the panel
No 26 tapestry needle
Gift tag, for suppliers see page 48

CARDS AND STATIONERY COMPENDIUM

The motifs for the two cards and the stationery compendium are stitched in the same way. Note that it is important to avoid excessive overstitching on the back, as this causes unsightly lumps to show on the right side. Prepare the fabric, marking the centre lines of each design with basting stitches. Complete the cross stitching, using two strands of cotton in the needle throughout. Steam press on the wrong side when complete.

Iron the interfacing to the back of the embroidery, and trim both to measure about 12mm (½in) larger all around than the cut-out window. Position the embroidery behind the window. Open out the self-adhesive mount and centre the embroidery behind the aperture.

Fold the card and press firmly to secure. Some cards may require a dab of glue to ensure a secure and neat finish.

GIFT TAGS

The designs for the lily, the passion flower and the *lavatera* gift tags are simply a single flower taken from each of the larger designs. For each, use one strand of thread in the needle for both cross stitch

LILY ◀		DMC	ANCHOR	MADEIRA
▆	Brown	898	360	2006
Z	Very deep yellow	741	304	0201
↖	Deep yellow	742	303	0107
→	Dark orange	900	333	0208
←	Orange	946	332	0207
⊞	Light orange	970	316	0204
•	Dark green	3051	846	1508
⊏	Green	3363	262	1602
K	Pale green	3364	260	1603
⋈	Yellow	743	297	0113

Note: bks stamens in brown, and stems in dark green.

and backstitch. Embroider from the centre. Steam press the embroidery on the wrong side.

Iron the interfacing to the back of the embroidery, and trim both to measure 6mm (¼in) larger all around than the cut-out window. This will prevent the mounted picture from wrinkling. Position the embroidery behind the window.

Open out the self-adhesive mount and centre the embroidery behind the aperture.

Fold the card and press firmly to secure. Some cards may require a dab of glue to ensure a secure and neat finish.

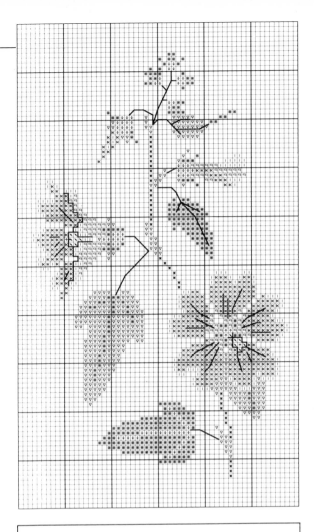

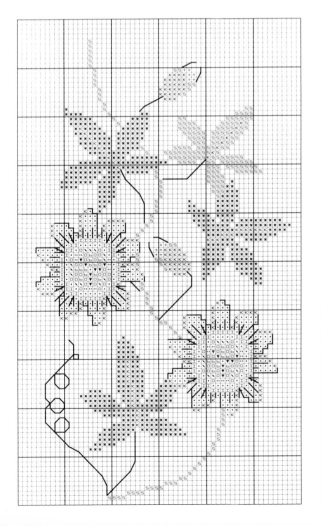

LAVATERA ▲		DMC	ANCHOR	MADEIRA
↖	Lemon	727	293	0110
✳	Dark green	3051	846	1508
▽	Mid green	3363	262	1602
⊡	Pale green	3053	859	1510
÷	Light grey green	644	830	1907
↑	Dark red	915	89	0705
⊟	Purplish pink	3607	87	0708
⊠	Pink	3608	86	0709
Ⅰ	Pale pink	3609	85	0710

Note: bks around the centres of the flowers in brown* (used for bks only), the stalk of the top bud in dark green, all other stalks and veins of top leaf in pale green, and the markings on the petals in dark red; the veins of the small leaf worked in pale green are stitched in light grey green.

PASSION FLOWER ◀		DMC	ANCHOR	MADEIRA
•	Ecru	Ecru	926	Ecru
↖	Yellow	743	297	0113
☐	Navy	939	127	1009
▼	Purplish brown	315	896	0810
⠢	Reddish brown	221	897	0811
✳	Dark green	890	879	1314
S	Green	3363	262	1602
⊔	Yellowish green	471	266	1501
K	Pale green	368	240	1310
⊞	Light green	3364	260	1603
Ⅰ	Purple	552	101	0713

Note: bks the tips of the buds in light green, all stems and tendrils in green, and the fringe around the centre of the flower in purple.

Tea Cosy

This elegant tea cosy, embroidered with lace-cap hydrangeas in delicate pastel shades, will make teatime extra special. Alternatively, you might like to stitch this attractive design as a framed picture, perhaps using fabric with a higher count.

TEA COSY

YOU WILL NEED

For the Tea Cosy, measuring 28cm × 33cm
(11in × 13in):

*Two pieces 38cm × 42cm (15in × 16½in) of
cream, 14-count Aida fabric
70cm (¾yd) of glazed cotton lining, 115cm (45in)
wide, of a colour chosen to tone with the design
46cm (½yd) of thick cotton/nylon wadding, 90cm
(1yd) wide
Stranded embroidery cotton in the colours given
in the panel
No24 tapestry needle
Matching sewing thread*

•

THE EMBROIDERY

Take one of the pieces of Aida and prepare the
fabric by marking the horizontal and vertical centre
lines with basting stitches. Start to embroider from
the centre of the design. Use three strands of cotton
in the needle for the cross stitch and two strands
for the backstitch. Steam press on the wrong side
when complete.

MAKING THE TEA COSY

After the embroidery has been completed, cut both
pieces of Aida together to form a dome shape. Cut
two pieces of lining to the same shape as the Aida,
and repeat with the wadding.

From the remaining lining fabric, cut two strips
8cm (3in) wide and 115cm (45in) long, for the frill.
Join the two long strips of lining at the narrow end,
to make one long strip. Press the seam open. Fold
the strip in half lengthwise and press. Stitch along
the raw edge to form pleats.

Matching raw edges, pin the frill around the
dome shape of the embroidered piece of Aida, on
the right side. Place the back of the tea cosy over
the embroidered front piece, sandwiching the frill
between the two. Baste all around the shaped edge,
and machine stitch. Turn right side out.

Take the two pieces of lining, right sides facing,
and sandwich the lining between the two pieces of
wadding. Baste and machine around, leaving the
bottom edge open. Insert the pad thus formed into
the main cover. Turn in the edges and slip stitch
all around the bottom.

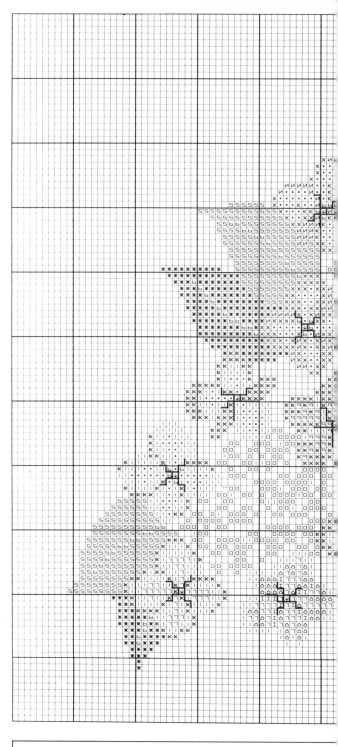

LACECAP HYDRANGEA ▲		DMC	ANCHOR	MADEIRA
•	Cream	746	275	0101
▢	Blue blend †	798	131	0911
		340	118	0902
		775	128	1001
	† 1 strand of each			
○	Blue	341	117	0901
И	Light blue	3325	159	1002
✕	Pale blue	775	128	1001

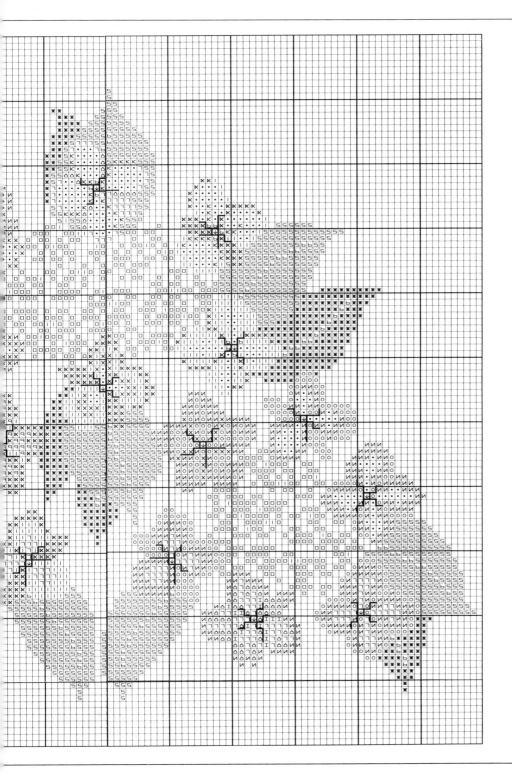

		DMC	ANCHOR	MADEIRA			DMC	ANCHOR	MADEIRA	
↓	Sky blue	809	130	0909	🖰 Deep pink		3607	87	0708	*Note: bks lines*
✳	Dark green	3362	862	1601	⊠ Pink		3608	86	0709	*separating petals of the*
🇸	Green	3346	817	1407	⊡ Pale pink		3609	85	0710	*blue flowers in dark*
🇧	Light green	3364	260	1603	Dark grey*		413	401	1713	*grey*, lines separating*
🇰	Yellowish green	472	264	1414	Grey*		317	400	1714	*petals of the pink*
🇮	Mauve	554	96	0711	Black*		310	403	Black	*flowers in grey*, and*
△	Light mauve	210	108	0802						*flower centres in black**
🇶	Pale mauve	211	342	0801						*(all used for bks only).*

Trinket Box

The fragile flower of love-in-a-mist
or *Nigella*, attracting a honey
bee, makes a delicate inset for
this rosewood trinket box.

TRINKET BOX

YOU WILL NEED

For the Trinket Box, with a lid measuring
10cm (4in) in diameter:

15cm (6in) square of cream, 18-count Aida fabric
15cm (6in) square of iron-on interfacing
Stranded embroidery cotton in the colours given
in the panel
No 26 tapestry needle
A trinket box; these are available in wood, hand-
cut lead crystal, silver-plate and porcelain, in a
variety of colours (for suppliers, see page 48) – you
may wish to choose a bowl in a colour to match
one of the colours in the embroidery

●

THE EMBROIDERY

Find the centre point on your square of Aida and,
beginning from the centre of the pattern, embroider
the flower motif, using two strands of cotton in
the needle for the cross stitch and for all the backstitching in green. For the delicate backstitching on
the bee's wings and body, use only one thread.
When working the cross stitch on the bee's wings,
I used one thread of stranded cotton together with
a strand of Kreinik Blending Filament. This gives
the wings a translucent appearance.

Steam press on the wrong side, but prevent the
iron from coming into direct contact with the blending filament.

ASSEMBLING THE TRINKET BOX

Iron the interfacing to the back of the embroidery.
Take the acetate inset from the lid of your bowl and
place it over the embroidery. This will enable
you to centre the motif within the circular space
available. Using the acetate as a template, draw
around it with a soft pencil. Cut around the circle
with a sharp pair of scissors, and complete the
assembly, following the manufacturer's instructions.

NIGELLA ▶	DMC	ANCHOR	MADEIRA
⊥ Grey	413	401	1713
⠿ Pale grey	762	234	1804
+ BF100 (Kreinik Blending Filament 100)			
Z Yellow brown	783	307	2211
◣ Yellow	726	295	0109
‖ Light yellow brown	676	891	2208
◤ Navy	823	150	1008
▢ Light navy	791	941	0904
☒ Pale blue	794	175	0907
⊟ Very pale blue	800	129	0908
↓ Dark blue	792	940	0905
⋀ Blue	793	121	0906
⊏ Dark green	580	267	1608
⊑ Green	581	266	1609
⊔ Pale green	472	264	1414

Note: bks bee's body in yellow brown, stamens in green, bee's
wings, legs and antennae in grey, and the centre of the flower
in navy, and leaves in dark green.

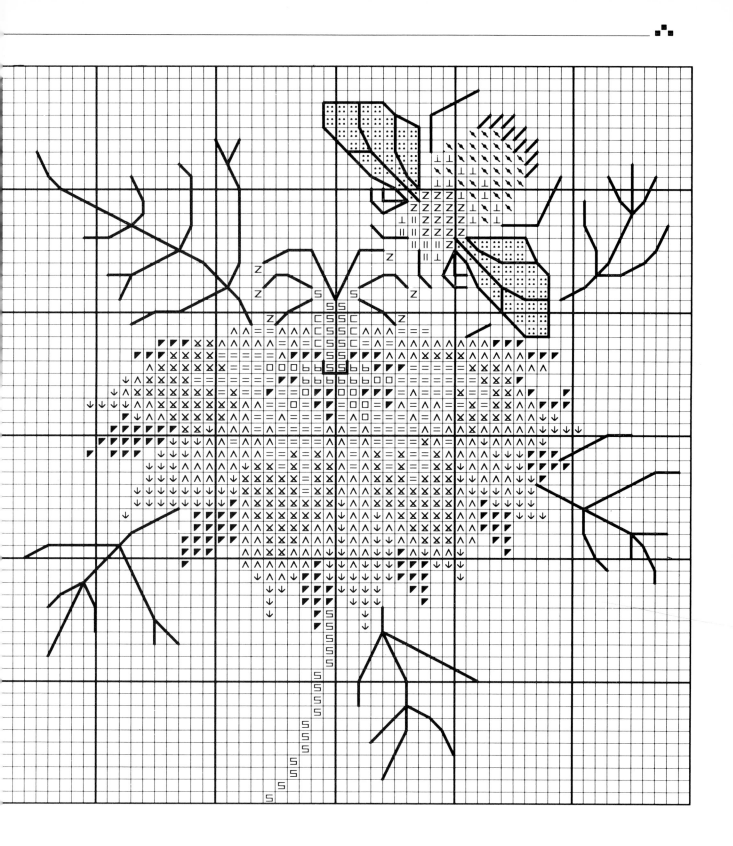

ACKNOWLEDGEMENTS

I should like to thank my mother, Violet Watts, who made up or assembled all the embroidered articles illustrated in this book, and who patiently recorded the various steps she took and processes she employed for inclusion in the instructions for finishing the projects.

I should also like to thank Betty Haste for all her help in finding fresh and perfect specimens of garden flowers for me to work from, and for checking patterns and proofs at all stages of the preparation of this book.

My thanks are also due to Pauline and Anne of the Kaleidoscope needlework and craft materials shop, The Square, Codsall, Staffordshire, who have followed the progress of this book with such interest and have always been at hand with practical help and suggestions.

My acknowledgements would not be complete without a sincere thank you to Alan Lord, Business and Personal Developments, for his advice and technical help with the transfer of my patterns to computer, always given with such patience and good humour.

Finally, I must express my appreciation to friends and neighbours who followed the creation of these designs with such interest and gave me so much encouragement.

SUPPLIERS

The following mail order company has supplied some of the basic items needed for making up the projects in this book:

Framecraft Miniatures Limited
372/376 Summer Lane
Hockley
Birmingham, B19 3QA
England
Telephone (021) 359 4442

Addresses for Framecraft stockists worldwide
Ireland Needlecraft Pty Ltd.
2-4 Keppel Drive
Hallam, Victoria 3803
Australia

Danish Art Needlework
PO Box 442, Lethbridge
Alberta T1J 3Z1
Canada

Sanyei Imports
PO Box 5, Hashima Shi
Gifu 501-62
Japan

The Embroidery Shop
286 Queen Street
Masterton
New Zealand

Anne Brinkley Designs Inc.
246 Walnut Street
Newton
Mass. 02160
USA

S A Threads and Cottons Ltd.
43 Somerset Road
Cape Town
South Africa

For information on your nearest stockist of embroidery cotton, contact the following:

DMC

UK
DMC Creative World Limited
62 Pullman Road
Wigston
Leicester, LE8 2DY
Telephone: 0533 811040

USA
The DMC Corporation
Port Kearney Bld.
10 South Kearney
N.J. 07032-0650
Telephone: 201 589 0606

AUSTRALIA
DMC Needlecraft Pty
P.O. Box 317
Earlswood 2206
NSW 2204
Telephone: 02599 3088

COATS AND ANCHOR

UK
Kilncraigs Mill
Alloa
Clackmannanshire
Scotland, FK10 1EG
Telephone: 0259 723431

USA
Coats & Clark
P.O. Box 27067
Dept CO1
Greenville
SC 29616
Telephone: 803 234 0103

AUSTRALIA
Coats Patons Crafts
Thistle Street
Launceston
Tasmania 7250
Telephone: 00344 4222

MADEIRA

UK
Madeira Threads (UK) Limited
Thirsk Industrial Park
York Road, Thirsk
N. Yorkshire, YO7 3BX
Telephone: 0845 524880

USA
Madeira Marketing Limited
600 East 9th Street
Michigan City
IN 46360
Telephone: 219 873 1000

AUSTRALIA
Penguin Threads Pty Limited
25-27 Izett Street
Prahran
Victoria 3181
Telephone: 03529 4400